LEARN SQL
BY EXAMPLES

SERGEY SKUDAEV

ISBN-13: 978-1546996347
ISBN-10: 1546996346

CONTENTS

INTRODUCTION

This book is for beginners and intermediates.

SQL stands for Structured Query Language. SQL is designed for managing data held in a relational database management system (RDBMS). The relational database is based on the relational model. In the relational database, each record in one table is linked to corresponding record(s) in the other table(s). The records´ ids are used to link related records

SQL is a standard way to manipulate a relational database data and any programmer of any computer language should know SQL. Even though it is standard, there are slightly different SQL "dialects" for different databases. In this book, I provide SQL query examples that I tested on MySQL, Oracle and MS Access.

A database is an application that stores data in organized data sets and manages data storage, retrieval and modification. In the relational database, data is stored in tables. Each table holds many records. Each record contains many fields and is identified with an ID that is the primary key of the record. For example, this is a computer courses table. The primary key is courseid field.

courseid	coursename	hours	cost
1	Visual Basic	360	1999.95
2	Java	500	2999.95
3	C++	550	3999.95
4	PHP	300	999.95
5	HTML	200	699.95
6	Pearl	300	1699.95
7	CSS	400	899.95
8	Assembly	400	1699.95

9	JavaScript	200	999.95
10	Python	300	999.95
12	Unix	700	1000

In our tutorial, we will use a computer school database. Tables in the database are linked. There are three types of relationships between linked tables.

> One to one
> One to many
> Many to many.

A one to one relationship is observed when one record in one table is related to only one record in another table. For example, one order record in the ORDER table is related to a one order details record in the OrderDetails table.

A one to many relationship is observed when one record in one table is related to many records in another table. In our school database, I created a "teachers" table and a "cars" table. One teacher may have a few cars, but each car can belong to only one teacher.

cid	teacherid	cmake	cyear
1	1	Ford	2007
2	1	Toyota	2012
3	2	Mercury	2003
4	2	Lexus	2011
5	3	Nissan	2010
6	4	Mazda	2009

The cars table has a primary key cid and a foreign key teacherid. The teacherid field links a cars table records to a teachers table record.

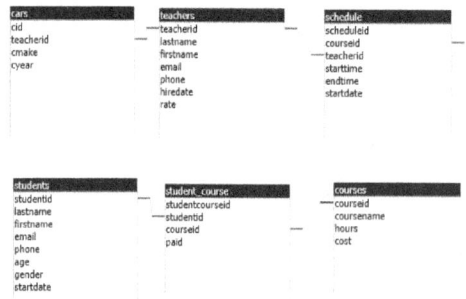

This figure displays relationships between all tables in our school database.

A student may take many computer courses and the same computer course can be taken by many students. The relationship between students and courses is MANY TO MANY. To implement a "MANY TO MANY" relationship we have to create a third table student_course. It will hold studentid and courseid as foreign keys and link student records with course records.

A relationship between the teachers table and the courses table is also "MANY TO MANY" because one teacher may teach many courses and the same course may be taught by many teachers. The schedule table has a foreign key for teacher and course records and links teachers and courses tables.

To practice SQL with this book you may use MySQL, Oracle or MS Access database.

First, you need to create tables and insert data, so that later you can use these tables to learn SQL with this book.

I provided Create Table statements so that you can create tables in any database mentioned above: MySQL, Oracle and MS Access.

You can find Create Table statements in the Appendix of the book or download a txt file from the link at the end of the book.

You can copy and paste these create table statements. When database and tables will be created, you can copy and paste inserts statements with the data to fill all the tables.

If you do not want to recreate the tables on your PC, you can use my web page for practice.

www.learn-coding.today/learn_sql.php

My website server has all the tables and data that are used for this book.

SIMPLE SELECT STATEMENT

To display data from all fields and all records of the courses table use the following query:

SELECT * FROM courses

Output:

courseid	coursename	hours	cost
1	Visual Basic	360	1999.95
2	Java	500	2999.95
3	C++	550	3999.95
4	PHP	300	999.95
5	HTML	200	699.95
6	Pearl	300	1699.95
7	CSS	400	899.95

8	Assembly	400	1699.95
9	JavaScript	200	999.95
10	Python	300	999.95
12	Unix	700	1000

You will get the same result if you list all table fields in the SELECT clause.

SELECT courseid, coursename, hours, cost FROM courses.

If you do not want to display values from all fields you should list only those fields that you need. Besides, you can choose by which field or fields you want to sort records. For that you should add ORDER BY key words.

SELECT courseid, coursename, hours, cost
FROM courses
ORDER BY coursename

Output:

courseid	coursename	hours	cost
8	Assembly	400	1699.95
3	C++	550	3999.95
7	CSS	400	899.95
5	HTML	200	699.95
2	Java	500	2999.95
9	JavaScript	200	999.95
6	Pearl	300	1699.95
4	PHP	300	999.95
10	Python	300	999.95
12	Unix	700	1000
1	Visual Basic	360	1999.95

SELECT courseid, coursename, hours, cost
FROM courses
ORDER BY cost, coursename

Output:

courseid	coursename	hours	cost
5	HTML	200	699.95
7	CSS	400	899.95

9	JavaScript	200	999.95
4	PHP	300	999.95
10	Python	300	999.95
12	Unix	700	1000
8	Assembly	400	1699.95
6	Pearl	300	1699.95
1	Visual Basic	360	1999.95
2	Java	500	2999.95
3	C++	550	3999.95

By default, records are sorted by fields included in the ORDER BY clause in ascending order. If you want to sort in descending order, you have to add the DESC key word.

SELECT courseid, coursename, hours, cost
FROM courses
ORDER BY cost desc, coursename

Output:

courseid	coursename	hours	cost
3	C++	550	3999.95
2	Java	500	2999.95
1	Visual Basic	360	1999.95
8	Assembly	400	1699.95
6	Pearl	300	1699.95
12	Unix	700	1000
9	JavaScript	200	999.95
4	PHP	300	999.95
10	Python	300	999.95
7	CSS	400	899.95
5	HTML	200	699.95

INSERT STATEMENT

When you inserted records in your database tables with insert statements downloaded from my website, you saw how the inset statement looked. It starts with INSERT INTO keywords and then a table name is required.

If you inserting a value into each existing column, then you do not have to list column names.

For example:

```
INSERT INTO courses
VALUES (1, 'SQL', 400, 399.95)
```

Strings and date data type values are enclosed in single quotation marks. Numeric values are not enclosed.

You may insert values only in a few columns. Then you must list the column names.

```
INSERT INTO courses(courseid, coursename, cost)
VALUES (1, 'Java', 399.95)
or
INSERT INTO courses(courseid, coursename, hours)
VALUES (1,
    'Java',
    200)
or
INSERT INTO courses (coursename)
VALUES ('SQL')
```

This statement will work in MySQL because MySQL will assign a value to courseid incremented by 1. For Oracle, this statement will not work because Oracle does not have auto number data type or attribute. You have to include courseid in the field list.

```
INSERT INTO courses (courseid, coursename)
VALUES (courses_seq.nextval,'SQL')
```

courses_seq.nextval is a sequence next value, assuming that the sequence courses_seq was created before. The courses_seq object will remember the id of the record that was inserted the last time and courses_seq.nextval will assign to the new id a next value incremented by 1. You will learn how to create a sequence in the appendix. Update, delete and insert statements are easy to understand. Much more complicated is the SELECT statement. How to write a correct select statement is described in the rest of the book.

UPDATE STATEMENT

To update data in a table, an update query is used. Let say, we want to change the cost of the Pearl course.

Then we can execute the following query:

UPDATE courses SET cost=1299.95 WHERE coursename='Pearl"
Or we can change hours for few courses.

UPDATE courses SET hours=500 WHERE coursename='HTML' or coursename='PHP'

We can update all fields.

UPDATE courses SET coursename='SQL', hours=300, cost=399.95 WHERE cousename='CSS'

DELETE STATEMENT.

To delete records from a table we can execute the following query:

DELETE FROM courses.

All courses will be deleted. Do not execute such query!
To delete a specific record we can use a condition in the WHERE clause:

DELETE FROM courses WHERE cousename='HTML'

Only the HTML course will be deleted.

COMPLEX SELECT STATEMENTS

String Functions

SELECT firstname,
      lastname,

```
       phone
FROM teachers
WHERE firstname='Michael'
ORDER BY LENGTH(lastname);
```

Output:

firstname	lastname	phone
Michael	Ross	910-092-3746
Michael	Kelly	727-098-1237
Michael	Murphy	910-987-1234

LENGTH function returns the number of characters in the string.

```
SELECT firstname,
     lastname
FROM students
WHERE LENGTH(firstname) > LENGTH(lastname);
```

Output:

firstname	lastname
Michael	Petrov
Michael	Holden

SUBSTR (string, position, length) function returns a substring of a string starting from a position and with the length that is equal to the second parameter if it is present. If it is not present, SUBSTR function returns all the remaining characters of the string. For example, SUBSTR('Jefferson', 1, 1) will return J.

SUBSTR ('Jefferson,4, 3) will return 'fer' and SUBSTR('Jefferson', 7) will return 'son'.

```
SELECT firstname,
     lastname
FROM teachers
WHERE SUBSTR(firstname, 1, 1)='J';
```

(If a first name starts with a 'J' the record is qualified for the query.)

Output:

firstname	lastname
John	Smith
John	Jefferson
James	Barry
Julia	Williams
John	Niven

```
SELECT firstname,
     lastname
FROM teachers
WHERE SUBSTR(lastname, 3,1)='r';
```

If the third character in the lastname is 'r' the record is qualified for the query.

Output:

firstname	lastname
James	Barry
Michael	Murphy
Christine	Merry
Greg	Gerald
Norm	Karon

```
SELECT INSTR(firstname, 'chael') AS POSITION
FROM students
WHERE lastname='Petrov';
```

Output:
Position
3

INSTR function returns a starting position of a substring in a string.
```
SELECT INSTR(firstname, 'el') AS POSITION
FROM students
WHERE lastname='Petrov';
```

Output:
Position
6

Aggregate Functions

Aggregate functions (COUNT, AVG, MAX, MIN, SUM) perform calculations on a set of values.

Some aggregate function names are different for different databases. See database manual for details.

For MySQL (http://dev.mysql.com/doc/refman/5.1/en/group-by-functions.html)

Oracle list of aggregate function (http://docs.oracle.com/cd/B19306_01/server.102/b14200/functions001.htm)

Find which course is the most expensive?

```
SELECT coursename
FROM courses
WHERE cost =
   (SELECT MAX (cost)
    FROM courses);
```

Output:
coursename
C++

Find which course is the least expensive?

```
SELECT coursename
FROM courses
WHERE cost =
   (SELECT MIN (cost)
    FROM courses);
```

Output:
coursename
HTML

Which course has higher cost per hour?
```
SELECT coursename
FROM courses
WHERE cost/hours =
   (SELECT MAX(cost/hours)
```

FROM courses);

Output:
coursename
C++

Which course has lowest cost per hour?

SELECT coursename
FROM courses
WHERE cost/hours =
    (SELECT MIN(cost/hours)
    FROM courses);

Output:
coursename
Unix

Find average cost:

SELECT AVG(cost)
FROM courses;

Output:
AVG(cost)
1636.31816517223

You can use the ROUND function to round the average cost. The ROUND function accepts column name and number of decimals. If the number of decimals is omitted, 0 is assumed.

SELECT ROUND(AVG(cost))
FROM courses

Output:
1636

SELECT ROUND(AVG(cost),2)
FROM courses

Output:
ROUND(AVG(cost),2)
1636.32

How much do all courses cost?

```
SELECT ROUND(SUM(cost))
FROM courses
```

Output:
ROUND(SUM(cost))
17999

```
SELECT ROUND(SUM(cost),2) FROM courses
```

Output:
ROUND(SUM(cost),2)
17999.50

Find courses that cost less than average.

```
SELECT coursename,
     cost
FROM courses
WHERE cost <
   (SELECT AVG(cost)
    FROM courses)
ORDER BY coursename
```

Output:

coursename	cost
CSS	899.95
HTML	699.95
JavaScript	999.95
PHP	999.95
Python	999.95
Unix	1000

How many students attended computer school?

```
SELECT COUNT(*)
FROM students
```

Output:
COUNT(*)
12

Find a standard deviation of grades for a student.

```
SELECT STD(grade)
FROM test_grades
WHERE studentid=17
```

STD function is valid for MySQL only. For Oracle you should use the STDDEV function.

Output:
STD(grade)
12.3884

Group By Function

Group By function requires an aggregate function such as COUNT, AVG, MAX, MIN, and SUM.

```
SELECT age,
    COUNT(*)
FROM students
GROUP BY age;
```

Output:
age	COUNT(*)
20	1
21	1
23	2
25	4
27	1
30	3

You cannot include lastname or firstname columns in the query above, because only field that used in GROUP BY clause can be included in

SELECT with aggregate function.

If you try to run in Oracle the following query:

```
SELECT lastname, age,
    COUNT(*)
FROM students
GROUP BY age;
```

You will get error:

```
ORA-00979: not a GROUP BY expression
00979. 00000 - "not a GROUP BY expression"
*Cause:
*Action:
Error at Line: 1 Column: 8
```

How many cars were made per each year?

```
SELECT cyear,
    COUNT(cid)
FROM cars
GROUP BY cyear;
```

Output:

cyear	COUNT(cid)
2003	1
2004	1
2006	1
2007	3
2008	1
2009	3
2010	2
2011	1
2012	5

Find a year in which at least 3 cars were made.

```
SELECT cyear,
    COUNT(cid)
FROM cars
GROUP BY cyear
HAVING COUNT(cid) > 2;
```

Output:

cyear	COUNT(cid)
2007	3
2009	3
2012	5

Which students' age is between 20 and 25 years?

```
SELECT firstname,
    lastname,
    age
FROM students
WHERE age BETWEEN 20 AND 25;
```

Output:

firstname	lastname	age
Michael	Petrov	21
Michael	Johnson	25
John	Williams	25
Holly	Michaels	20
Cindy	Brown	23
Julia	Barklay	23
Alison	Cremette	25
James	Folkner	25

```
SELECT firstname,
    lastname,  age
FROM students
WHERE age > 20
  AND age < 25;
```

Output:

firstname	lastname	age
Michael	Petrov	21
Cindy	Brown	23
Julia	Barklay	23

How many students are males?

```
SELECT COUNT (studentid) AS Males
```

```
FROM students
WHERE gender='male';
```

Output:
Males
7

How many students are females who are younger than 25?

```
SELECT COUNT(studentid) AS Females
FROM students
WHERE gender='female'
  AND age < 25;
```

Output:
Females
3

Find female students who are younger than 25 and whose start dates are before 06/12/10?

```
SELECT firstname,
    lastname
FROM students
WHERE gender='female'
  AND age < 25
  AND startdate < '2010-12-06';
```
Output:
firstname lastname
Holly   Michaels

Find female students who are younger than 25 and whose start dates are before 06/12/10?

```
SELECT firstname,
    lastname
FROM students
WHERE gender='female'
  AND age < 25
  AND startdate < '2010-12-06';
```

Output:
firstname lastname

Molly   James

Find male students who are younger than 25 and whose start dates are before 06/12/10?

```
SELECT firstname,
     lastname
FROM students
WHERE gender='male'
 AND age < 25
 AND startdate < '2010-12-06';
```

Output:

firstname	lastname
Lee	George
Michael	Holden
Ryan	Brown

```
SELECT firstname,
     lastname
FROM teachers
ORDER BY lastname;
```

Output:

firstname	lastname
James	Barry
Greg	Gerald
John	Jameson
Norm	Karon
Michael	Kelly
Christine	Merry
Michael	Murphy
John	Niven
Michael	Ross
John	Smith
Julia	Williams

Join Two Tables: Teachers and Cars.

The relationship between these two tables is ONE TO MANY. One teacher may have many cars and a car may belong to only one teacher. The cars table has a teacherid field to link a car record to a teacher record.

Find which cars belong to which teacher.

To construct the query, you have to list all the fields you want with the table name in front of the field name. That way the system will know the field of which table your mean.

SELECT teachers.firstname, teachers.lastname, cars.cmake, cars.cyear. .
Then you have to include "FROM" keyword and a list of table names separated with comma.
FROM teachers, cars
Then you have to say how these tables are linked. You do it in the WHERE clause.

WHERE teachers.teacherid = cars.teacherid

Then you can add additional conditions or sorting keywords.

SELECT teachers.firstname,
    teachers.lastname,
    cars.cmake,
    cars.cyear
FROM teachers,
    cars
WHERE teachers.teacherid=cars.teacherid
ORDER BY teachers.lastname;

You can substitute table names with letters to make the query shorter and more readable.
In the FROM clause you add a character that you are going to use as a table name alias.

FROM teachers t, cars c

Then you put table aliases in front of each field: t.teacher, c.cmake .

SELECT t.firstname,
    t.lastname,
    c.cmake,
    c.cyear
FROM teachers t,
    cars c

WHERE t.teacherid=c.teacherid
ORDER BY t.lastname

INNER JOIN

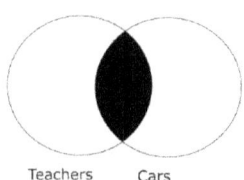

Teachers   Cars

The INNER JOIN keyword selects records that have matching values in both tables
The syntax of INNER JOIN is that:

SELECT column_name(s)
FROM table1
INNER JOIN table2 ON table1.column=table2.column

Let us write a join query using teachers and cars tables:

SELECT t.firstname,
    t.lastname,
    c.cmake,
    c.cyear
FROM teachers t
INNER JOIN cars c ON t.teacherid=c.teacherid
ORDER BY t.lastname;

Output:

firstname	lastname	cmake	cyear
James	Barry	Nissan	2010
Greg	Gerald	Chevrolet	2009
Greg	Gerald	Jaguar	2010
John	Jameson	Porsche	2009
John	Jameson	Mercury	2003
John	Jameson	Lexus	2011
Norm	Karon	Saturn	2012
Norm	Karon	Volvo	2007
Michael	Kelly	BMW	2006
Christine	Merry	Pontiac	2008
Michael	Murphy	Mazda	2009

John	Niven	Hyundai	2012
Michael	Ross	Acura	2012
Michael	Ross	Hummer	2004
John	Smith	Ford	2007
John	Smith	Suzuki	2012
John	Smith	Toyota	2012
Julia	Williams	Honda	2007

Which cars do John Jameson have?

```
SELECT t.firstname,
    t.lastname,
    c.cmake,
    c.cyear
FROM teachers t
INNER JOIN cars c ON t.teacherid=c.teacherid
AND t.lastname='Jameson'
ORDER BY c.cmake;
```

Output:

firstname	lastname	cmake	cyear
John	Jameson	Lexus	2011
John	Jameson	Mercury	2003
John	Jameson	Porsche	2009

Who has BMW?

```
SELECT t.firstname,
    t.lastname,
    c.cmake,
    c.cyear
FROM teachers t
INNER JOIN cars c ON t.teacherid=c.teacherid
AND c.cmake='BMW'
ORDER BY t.lastname;
```

Output:

| firstname | lastname | cmake | cyear |
| Michael | Kelly | BMW | 2006 |

Who has more than two cars?

```
SELECT t.lastname
FROM teachers t
INNER JOIN cars c ON t.teacherid=c.teacherid
AND
  (SELECT COUNT(cid)
   FROM cars
   WHERE teacherid=t.teacherid) > 2;
```

Output:

lastname
Smith
Smith
Jameson
Jameson
Smith
Jameson

The same teacher names were selected twice. To fix the problem we have to add the DISTINCT keyword.

```
SELECT DISTINCT t.lastname
FROM teachers t
INNER JOIN cars c ON t.teacherid=c.teacherid
AND
  (SELECT COUNT(cid)
   FROM cars
   WHERE teacherid=t.teacherid) > 2;
```

Output:
lastname
Smith
Jameson

Who has the oldest car?

```
SELECT t.lastname,
       c.cmake,
       c.cyear
FROM teachers t
INNER JOIN cars c ON t.teacherid=c.teacherid
AND c.cyear =
```

```
(SELECT MIN(cyear)
 FROM cars);
```

Output:

lastname	cmake	cyear
Jameson	Mercury	2003

Who has new cars?

```
SELECT t.lastname,
    c.cmake,
    c.cyear
FROM teachers t
INNER JOIN cars c ON t.teacherid=c.teacherid
AND c.cyear =
 (SELECT MAX(cyear)
  FROM cars)
```

Output:

lastname	cmake	cyear
Smith	Toyota	2012
Niven	Hyundai	2012
Ross	Acura	2012
Karon	Saturn	2012
Smith	Suzuki	2012

How many cars does each teacher have?

```
SELECT t.lastname,
    COUNT(c.cid) AS "Number of cars"
FROM teachers t
INNER JOIN cars c ON t.teacherid=c.teacherid
GROUP BY t.lastname
```

Output:

lastname	Number of cars
Barry	1
Gerald	2
Jameson	3
Karon	2
Kelly	1
Merry	1
Murphy	1

Niven	1
Ross	2
Smith	3
Williams	1

OUTER JOIN

LEFT OUTER JOIN RIGHT OUTER JOIN

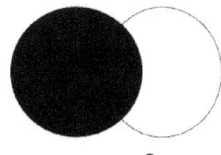 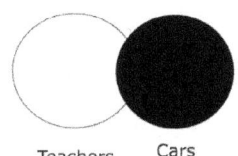

Teachers Cars   Teachers Cars

OUTER JOIN is used when not all records in the first table have corresponding records in the second table and it is required to display all records from the first table regardless of an existence of the corresponding records in the second one.

For example, we want to display teachers and their corresponding cars. Not all cars, but only those, which were made after 2010 year.

```
SELECT t.firstname,
    t.lastname,
    c.cmake,
    c.cyear
FROM teachers t
INNER JOIN cars c ON t.teacherid=c.teacherid
AND c.cyear > 2010
ORDER BY t.lastname;
```

Output:

firstname	lastname	cmake	cyear
John	Jameson	Lexus	2011
Norm	Karon	Saturn	2012
John	Niven	Hyundai	2012
Michael	Ross	Acura	2012
John	Smith	Toyota	2012
John	Smith	Suzuki	2012

If we are using INNER JOIN key words then only those teachers will be displayed whose cars were made after 2010. If we want to display all teachers regardless of year, when their cars were made and display cars that were made only after 2010, we have to use OUTER JOIN. Since we want to pull all the records from the left table, we have to use   LEFT OUTER JOIN.

```
SELECT t.firstname,
     t.lastname,
     c.cmake,
     c.cyear
FROM teachers t
LEFT OUTER JOIN cars c ON t.teacherid=c.teacherid
AND c.cyear > 2010
ORDER BY t.lastname;
```

Output:

firstname	lastname	cmake	cyear
James	Barry		
Greg	Gerald		
John	Jameson	Lexus	2011
Norm	Karon	Saturn	2012
Michael	Kelly		
Christine	Merry		
Michael	Murphy		
John	Niven	Hyundai	2012
Michael	Ross	Acura	2012
John	Smith	Toyota	2012
John	Smith	Suzuki	2012
Julia	Williams		

If we want to display all cars but only those teachers who were hired after 2010 and all cars, we must use RIGHT OUTER JOIN.

```
SELECT t.firstname,
     t.lastname,
     c.cmake,
     c.cyear
FROM teachers t
RIGHT OUTER JOIN cars c ON t.teacherid=c.teacherid
AND c.cyear > 2010
AND t.hiredate >2010
ORDER BY t.lastname;
```

Output:

firstname	lastname	cmake	cyear
		Ford	2007
		Nissan	2010
		Pontiac	2008
		Mazda	2009
		Chevrolet	2009
		Volvo	2007
		Porsche	2009
		Mercury	2003
		Honda	2007
		Jaguar	2010
		BMW	2006
		Hummer	2004
John	Niven	Hyundai	2012
John	Jameson	Lexus	2011
Norm	Karon	Saturn	2012
Michael	Ross	Acura	2012
John	Smith	Suzuki	2012
John	Smith	Toyota	2012

Join Three Tables.

To join three tables you have to join two tables and then consider these two tables as one. That way, it will be easier for you to understand how to join the third table.

Find which teachers teach which courses?

```
SELECT t.lastname,
       c.coursename
FROM (teachers t
    INNER JOIN schedule s ON t.teacherid=s.teacherid)
INNER JOIN courses c ON s.courseid=c.courseid;
```

First we join the teachers and schedule table. To stress it, I included these tables in parentheses. Then we join whatever is in parentheses with the third table. Parentheses are not required for MySQL or Oracle. For MS Access, parentheses are required.

```
SELECT t.lastname,
       c.coursename
```

FROM (teachers t
    INNER JOIN schedule s ON t.teacherid=s.teacherid)
INNER JOIN courses c ON s.courseid=c.courseid;

Output:

firstname	lastname	coursename
John	Smith	Java
Michael	Ross	Visual Basic
Michael	Murphy	PHP
Michael	Murphy	Pearl
Michael	Murphy	Python
Julia	Williams	HTML
Julia	Williams	CSS
James	Barry	C++
John	Niven	JavaScript
Greg	Gerald	Assembly
Christine	Merry	Visual Basic
Christine	Merry	Java
John	Jefferson	Visual Basic
John	Jefferson	Java
Julia	Williams	JavaScript
Julia	Williams	Python
Michael	Kelly	C++
Norm	Karon	C++

Which teachers teach Java?

SELECT DISTINCT t.firstname,
        t.lastname,
        c.coursename
FROM (teachers t
    INNER JOIN schedule s ON t.teacherid=s.teacherid)
INNER JOIN courses c ON s.courseid=c.courseid
AND c.coursename='Java'
ORDER BY t.lastname;

Output:

firstname	lastname	coursename
John	Jefferson	Java
Christine	Merry	Java
John	Smith	Java

Let us find which students study which courses

30

```
SELECT DISTINCT s.firstname,
          s.lastname,
          c.coursename
FROM students s
INNER JOIN student_course sc ON s.studentid=sc.studentid
INNER JOIN courses c ON sc.courseid=c.courseid
ORDER BY s.lastname,
      c.coursename;
```

Output:

firstname	lastname	coursename
Julia	Barklay	CSS
Julia	Barklay	Pearl
Julia	Barklay	Visual Basic
Ryan	Brown	HTML
Cindy	Brown	HTML
Ryan	Brown	JavaScript
Cindy	Brown	Unix
Cindy	Brown	Visual Basic
Alison	Cremette	Pearl
Alison	Cremette	PHP
Alison	Cremette	Visual Basic
James	Folkner	Pearl
James	Folkner	Python
Lee	George	C++
Lee	George	Pearl
Lee	George	Visual Basic
Michael	Holden	Java
Michael	Holden	Visual Basic
Molly	James	HTML
Molly	James	Java
Molly	James	Pearl
Michael	Johnson	C++
Michael	Johnson	Java
Michael	Johnson	Pearl
Holly	Michaels	Java
Holly	Michaels	JavaScript
Holly	Michaels	Pearl
Michael	Petrov	Java
Michael	Petrov	Visual Basic
John	Williams	Assembly
John	Williams	C++

John	Williams	JavaScript
John	Williams	Visual Basic

UNION

The UNION keyword joins any set of records that have the same number of fields (columns).

For example, we can write a query like:

```
SELECT firstname,
    lastname
FROM students
UNION
SELECT courseid,
    coursename
FROM courses;
```

Both halves of the query in UNION have the same number of columns but they are not related.

However the syntax of query is correct and we will get the following records:

firstname	lastname
Michael	Petrov
Michael	Johnson
John	Williams
Lee	George
Molly	James
Holly	Michaels
Cindy	Brown
Julia	Barklay
Alison	Cremette
James	Folkner
Michael	Holden
Ryan	Brown

1	Visual Basic
2	Java
3	C++
4	PHP
5	HTML

6	Pearl
7	CSS
8	Assembly
9	JavaScript
10	Python
11	Unix

This result is not very useful.

We may use the UNION to join students and teachers for the C++ course. It will make sense.

```
SELECT firstname,
    lastname
FROM students
WHERE studentid IN
  (SELECT DISTINCT s.studentid
   FROM students s
   INNER JOIN student_course sc ON s.studentid=sc.studentid
   INNER JOIN courses c ON sc.courseid=c.courseid
   AND c.coursename='C++')
UNION
SELECT firstname,
    lastname
FROM teachers
WHERE teacherid IN
  (SELECT DISTINCT t.teacherid
   FROM (teachers t
       INNER JOIN schedule s ON t.teacherid=s.teacherid)
   INNER JOIN courses c ON s.courseid=c.courseid
   AND c.coursename='C++');
```

Output:

firstname	lastname
Michael	Johnson
John	Williams
Lee	**George**
James	**Barry**
Michael	**Kelly**
Norm	**Karon**

Teachers are shown in bold.

The following query retrieves students who take C++:

```
SELECT DISTINCT s.studentid
FROM students s
INNER JOIN student_course sc ON s.studentid=sc.studentid
INNER JOIN courses c ON sc.courseid=c.courseid
AND c.coursename='C++';
```

The query retrieves the teachers who teach C++:

```
SELECT DISTINCT t.teacherid
    FROM (teachers t
        INNER JOIN schedule s ON t.teacherid=s.teacherid)
    INNER JOIN courses c ON s.courseid=c.courseid
    AND c.coursename='C++;
```

By UNION these two queries, we get both students and teachers who belong to C++ course.

Creating a monster query

Let us create a query that calculates how many students are taking each course

First, let us find how many students study Java.

```
SELECT COUNT(s.studentid) AS "java students"
FROM (students s
    INNER JOIN student_course sc ON s.studentid=sc.studentid)
INNER JOIN courses c ON sc.courseid=c.courseid
AND c.coursename='Java';
```

Output:
java students
5

Let us find how many students study Visual Basic.

```
SELECT COUNT(s.studentid) AS "VB students"
FROM (students s
    INNER JOIN student_course sc ON s.studentid=sc.studentid)
INNER JOIN courses c ON sc.courseid=c.courseid
AND c.coursename='Visual Basic';
```

Output:
VB students
7

Let us find how many students study C++

```
SELECT COUNT(s.studentid) AS "C++ students"
FROM (students s
    INNER JOIN student_course sc ON s.studentid=sc.studentid)
INNER JOIN courses c ON sc.courseid=c.courseid
AND c.coursename='C++';
```

Output:
C++ students
3

Since I am using MySQL for this book, I will not use parentheses anymore. If you use MS Access just remember to add parentheses.

Let us find how many students study JavaScript

```
SELECT COUNT(s.studentid) AS "JavaScript"
FROM students s
INNER JOIN student_course sc ON s.studentid=sc.studentid
INNER JOIN courses c ON sc.courseid=c.courseid
AND c.coursename='JavaScript';
```

Output:
JavaScript
3

How many students are learning HTML or PHP?

```
SELECT s.firstname,
    s.lastname,
    c.coursename
FROM students s
INNER JOIN student_course sc ON s.studentid=sc.studentid
INNER JOIN courses c ON sc.courseid=c.courseid
AND (c.coursename='HTML'
    OR c.coursename='PHP');
```

Output:

firstname	lastname	coursename
Ryan	Brown	HTML
Molly	James	HTML
Cindy	Brown	HTML
Alison	Cremette	PHP

It is important to understand why we enclosed c.coursename='HTML' OR c.coursename='PHP' in parentheses.

If we wanted to find students who study HTML and then students who study PHP, we would use two queries:

1.SELECT DISTINCT s.firstname,
             s.lastname,
             c.coursename
FROM students s
INNER JOIN student_course sc ON s.studentid=sc.studentid
INNER JOIN courses c ON sc.courseid=c.courseid
AND c.coursename='HTML';

Output:
firstname	lastname	coursename
Ryan	Brown	HTML
Cindy	Brown	HTML
Molly	James	HTML

2. SELECT DISTINCT s.firstname,
             s.lastname,
             c.coursename
FROM students s
INNER JOIN student_course sc ON s.studentid=sc.studentid
INNER JOIN courses c ON sc.courseid=c.courseid
AND c.coursename='PHP';

Output:
firstname	lastname	coursename
Alison	Cremette	PHP

Then we can combine those queries into one by using "AND (c.coursename='HTML' OR c.coursename='PHP'). "

Try to use it without parentheses:

SELECT DISTINCT s.firstname,

```
        s.lastname,
        c.coursename
FROM students s
INNER JOIN student_course sc ON s.studentid=sc.studentid
INNER JOIN courses c ON sc.courseid=c.courseid
AND c.coursename='HTML'
OR c.coursename='PHP';
```

Output:

firstname	lastname	coursename
Ryan	Brown	PHP
Michael	Petrov	PHP
John	Williams	PHP
Julia	Barklay	PHP
Alison	Cremette	PHP
Ryan	Brown	HTML
Lee	George	PHP
Holly	Michaels	PHP
James	Folkner	PHP
Cindy	Brown	PHP
Michael	Holden	PHP
Michael	Johnson	PHP
Molly	James	PHP
Cindy	Brown	HTML
Molly	James	HTML

Without parentheses, it will display the wrong records from students because this query is a combination of two different queries. The first is the same.

```
SELECT DISTINCT s.firstname,
        s.lastname,
        c.coursename
FROM students s
INNER JOIN student_course sc ON s.studentid=sc.studentid
INNER JOIN courses c ON sc.courseid=c.courseid
AND c.coursename='HTML'
```

And the second is different:

```
SELECT DISTINCT s.firstname,
        s.lastname,
        c.coursename
```

```
FROM students s
INNER JOIN student_course sc ON s.studentid=sc.studentid
INNER JOIN courses c ON sc.courseid=c.courseid
OR c.coursename='PHP';
```

Output:

firstname	lastname	coursename
Ryan	Brown	PHP
Ryan	Brown	JavaScript
Michael	Petrov	Java
Michael	Petrov	PHP
John	Williams	PHP
John	Williams	Assembly
Julia	Barklay	PHP
Julia	Barklay	CSS
Alison	Cremette	PHP
Alison	Cremette	Pearl
Ryan	Brown	HTML
Lee	George	C++
Lee	George	PHP
Holly	Michaels	Java
Holly	Michaels	PHP
Julia	Barklay	Visual Basic
James	Folkner	PHP
James	Folkner	Python
Cindy	Brown	Visual Basic
Cindy	Brown	PHP
Lee	George	Visual Basic
John	Williams	Visual Basic
Michael	Petrov	Visual Basic
Alison	Cremette	Visual Basic
Michael	Holden	Visual Basic
Michael	Holden	PHP
Michael	Holden	Java
Michael	Johnson	Java
Michael	Johnson	PHP
Molly	James	Java
Molly	James	PHP
Michael	Johnson	C++
John	Williams	C++
Cindy	Brown	HTML
Molly	James	HTML
Molly	James	Pearl

Michael	Johnson	Pearl
Lee	George	Pearl
Holly	Michaels	Pearl
James	Folkner	Pearl
Julia	Barklay	Pearl
Holly	Michaels	JavaScript
John	Williams	JavaScript

This method is used by hackers. For example, to login into a bank account a query like that is used.

```
SELECT *
FROM users
WHERE login='johns'
  AND password='supersecret';
```

A hacker can insert an additional piece of sql.

```
SELECT *
FROM users
WHERE login='johns'
  AND password='supersecret' or 1;
```

And the system will display all logins and passwords from the user table because 1 is always true. If you do not believe me, try the following query:

```
SELECT DISTINCT s.firstname,
        s.lastname,
        c.coursename
FROM students s
INNER JOIN student_course sc ON s.studentid=sc.studentid
INNER JOIN courses c ON sc.courseid=c.courseid
AND c.coursename='PHP'
  OR 1;
```

Or you can try

```
SELECT s.firstname,
      s.lastname,
      c.coursename
FROM students s
INNER JOIN student_course sc ON s.studentid=sc.studentid
INNER JOIN courses c ON sc.courseid=c.courseid
```

AND (c.coursename='HTML'
   OR 1);

And you will see all students and all courses.

Which teachers do not teach C++ and do not teach Java?

```
SELECT DISTINCT t.firstname,
            t.lastname
FROM teachers t
INNER JOIN schedule s ON t.teacherid = s.teacherid
AND s.courseid NOT IN
   (SELECT courseid
    FROM courses
    WHERE coursename='C++'
     OR coursename='Java')
ORDER BY t.lastname,
       t.firstname;
```

Output:
firstname	lastname
Greg	Gerald
John	Jefferson
Christine	Merry
Michael	Murphy
John	Niven
Michael	Ross
Julia	Williams

Why is this query not correct? John Niven teaches only JavaScript. Greg Gerald teaches only assembly, but John Jefferson and Christine Merry teach VB and Java. Michael Murphy teaches PHP, Pearl and Python. Michael Ross teaches VB. Julia Williams teaches HTML, CSS, JavaScript and Python. So, our query is correct for all teachers except John Jefferson and Christine Merry. Why it is not correct for them?

Because condition: WHERE s.courseid NOT in

 SELECT courseid

FROM courses

WHERE coursename='C++'

40

OR coursename='Java';

Is true for them even though their ids are linked to Java courseid only and are not linked to C ++ id. In WHERE clause we have OR. It means if one part of two parts is true the whole is true.

Let us substitute OR with AND.

```
SELECT DISTINCT t.firstname,
          t.lastname
FROM teachers t
INNER JOIN schedule s ON t.teacherid = s.teacherid
AND s.courseid NOT IN
   (SELECT courseid
    FROM courses
    WHERE coursename='C++'
     AND coursename='Java')
ORDER BY t.lastname,
       t.firstname;
```

The query will still not be correct because now it has excluded teachers who teach both C++ and Java.
And Jefferson will be included because he teaches only Java and does not teach C++.
Let us find teachers who teaches C++ or Java (either of the two)

```
SELECT DISTINCT t.firstname,
          t.lastname
FROM (teachers t
     INNER JOIN schedule s ON t.teacherid = s.teacherid)
INNER JOIN courses c ON s.courseid=c.courseid
AND ( c.coursename = 'C++' OR c.coursename = 'Java')
ORDER BY t.lastname;
```

Output:

firstname	lastname
James	Barry
John	Jefferson
Norm	Karon
Michael	Kelly
Christine	Merry
John	Smith

This query is correct.

Now we have to write a query that retrieves all teachers except these 6

```
SELECT DISTINCT firstname, lastname FROM teachers
WHERE teacherid NOT in
( SELECT DISTINCT t.teacherid
FROM teachers t INNER JOIN schedule s
ON t.teacherid = s.teacherid INNER JOIN courses c
ON s.courseid=c.courseid
AND
(c.coursename = 'C++' OR c.coursename = 'Java'))
ORDER BY lastname
```

Output:

firstname	lastname
Greg	Gerald
Michael	Murphy
John	Niven
Michael	Ross
Julia	Williams

Now our query retrieves the correct teachers. None of them teach Java or C++.

How many students learn HTML?

```
SELECT COUNT(s.studentid)
FROM students s,
    student_course sc
WHERE s.studentid=sc.studentid
  AND sc.courseid IN
    (SELECT courseid
    FROM courses
    WHERE coursename='HTML');
```

The same result can be accomplished with the following query:

```
SELECT COUNT(s.studentid)
FROM students s
INNER JOIN student_course sc ON s.studentid=sc.studentid
AND sc.courseid IN
    (SELECT courseid
```

```
FROM courses
WHERE coursename='HTML');
```

The result is 3

Now you can substitute HTML with the other courses and find how many students are taking each course.

```
SELECT COUNT(s.studentid)
FROM students s
INNER JOIN student_course sc ON s.studentid=sc.studentid
AND sc.courseid IN
  (SELECT courseid
   FROM courses
   WHERE coursename='Java');
```

The result is 5

```
SELECT COUNT(s.studentid)
FROM students s
INNER JOIN student_course sc ON s.studentid=sc.studentid
AND sc.courseid IN
  (SELECT courseid
   FROM courses
   WHERE coursename='C++');
```

The result is 3

Let us combine a query for total students and a query for the number of students taking C++

```
SELECT COUNT(studentid) AS TOTAL,

  (SELECT COUNT(s.studentid)
   FROM students s
   INNER JOIN student_course sc ON s.studentid=sc.studentid
   AND sc.courseid IN
     (SELECT courseid
      FROM courses
      WHERE coursename='C++')) AS CN
FROM students;
```

Output:

TOTAL   CN
12   3

Let us combine a query for total students, a query for number of students taking C++ and a query for number of students taking HTML.

SELECT COUNT(studentid) AS TOTAL,

  (SELECT COUNT(s.studentid)
  FROM students s
  INNER JOIN student_course sc ON s.studentid=sc.studentid
  AND sc.courseid IN
    (SELECT courseid
    FROM courses
    WHERE coursename='C++')) AS CN,

  (SELECT COUNT(s.studentid)
  FROM students s
  INNER JOIN student_course sc ON s.studentid=sc.studentid
  AND sc.courseid IN
    (SELECT courseid
    FROM courses
    WHERE coursename='HTML')) HTMLN
FROM students;

Output:
TOTAL   CN   HTMLN
12   3   3

Let us add to the previous query a query for number of students taking Java.

SELECT COUNT(studentid) AS TOTAL,

  (SELECT COUNT(s.studentid)
  FROM students s
  INNER JOIN student_course sc ON s.studentid=sc.studentid
  AND sc.courseid IN
    (SELECT courseid
    FROM courses
    WHERE coursename='C++')) AS CN,

  (SELECT COUNT(s.studentid)
  FROM students s

```
INNER JOIN student_course sc ON s.studentid=sc.studentid
AND sc.courseid IN
   (SELECT courseid
    FROM courses
    WHERE coursename='HTML')) AS HTMLN,

(SELECT COUNT(s.studentid)
 FROM students s
 INNER JOIN student_course sc ON s.studentid=sc.studentid
 AND sc.courseid IN
    (SELECT courseid
     FROM courses
     WHERE coursename='Java')) AS JN
FROM students;
```

Output:

TOTAL	CN	HTMLN	JN
12	3	3	5

Let us add to the previous query a query for number of students taking Visual Basic

```
SELECT COUNT(studentid) as TOTAL,
(SELECT COUNT(s.studentid)
FROM students s
INNER JOIN student_course sc
ON s.studentid=sc.studentid
AND sc.courseid in
(SELECT courseid
FROM courses
WHERE coursename='C++')) as CN,
(SELECT COUNT(s.studentid)
FROM students s
INNER JOIN student_course sc
ON s.studentid=sc.studentid
AND sc.courseid in
(SELECT courseid
FROM courses
WHERE coursename='HTML')) as HTMLN,
(SELECT COUNT(s.studentid)
FROM students s
INNER JOIN student_course sc
ON s.studentid=sc.studentid
```

```
AND sc.courseid in
(SELECT courseid
FROM courses
WHERE coursename='Java')) as JN,
(SELECT COUNT(s.studentid)
FROM students s INNER JOIN student_course sc
ON s.studentid=sc.studentid
AND sc.courseid in
(SELECT courseid
FROM courses
WHERE coursename='Visual Basic')) as VBN
FROM students
```

Output:

TOTAL	CN	HTMLN	JN	VBN
12	3	3	5	7

Let us add to the previous query a query for number of students taking PHP.

```
SELECT COUNT(studentid) as TOTAL,
(SELECT COUNT(s.studentid)
FROM students s INNER JOIN student_course sc
ON s.studentid=sc.studentid
AND sc.courseid in
(SELECT courseid
FROM courses
WHERE coursename='C++')) as CN,
(SELECT COUNT(s.studentid)
FROM students s INNER JOIN student_course sc
ON s.studentid=sc.studentid
AND sc.courseid in
(SELECT courseid
FROM courses
WHERE coursename='HTML')) as HTMLN,
(SELECT COUNT(s.studentid)
FROM students s INNER JOIN student_course sc
ON s.studentid=sc.studentid
AND sc.courseid in
(SELECT courseid
FROM courses
WHERE coursename='Java')) as JN,
```

```
(SELECT COUNT(s.studentid)
FROM students s INNER JOIN student_course sc
ON s.studentid=sc.studentid
AND sc.courseid in
(SELECT courseid
FROM courses
WHERE coursename='Visual Basic')) as VBN,
(SELECT COUNT(s.studentid)
FROM students s INNER JOIN student_course sc
ON s.studentid=sc.studentid
AND sc.courseid in
(SELECT courseid
FROM courses
WHERE coursename='PHP')) as PHPN
FROM students
```

Output:

TOTAL	CN	HTMLN	JN	VBN	PHPN
12	3	3	5	7	1

Let us add to the previous query queries for number of students taking each of the remaining courses.

```
SELECT COUNT(studentid) as TOTAL,
(SELECT COUNT(s.studentid)
FROM students s INNER JOIN student_course sc
ON s.studentid=sc.studentid
AND sc.courseid in
(SELECT courseid
FROM courses
WHERE coursename='C++')) as CN,
(SELECT COUNT(s.studentid)
FROM students s INNER JOIN student_course sc
ON s.studentid=sc.studentid
AND sc.courseid in
(SELECT courseid
FROM courses
WHERE coursename='HTML')) as HTMLN,
(SELECT COUNT(s.studentid)
FROM students s INNER JOIN student_course sc
ON s.studentid=sc.studentid
AND sc.courseid in
(SELECT courseid
```

FROM courses WHERE coursename='Java')) as JN,
(SELECT COUNT(s.studentid)
FROM students s INNER JOIN student_course sc
ON s.studentid=sc.studentid
AND sc.courseid in
(SELECT courseid
FROM courses
WHERE coursename='Visual Basic')) as VBN,
(SELECT COUNT(s.studentid)
FROM students s INNER JOIN student_course sc
ON s.studentid=sc.studentid
AND sc.courseid in
(SELECT courseid
FROM courses
WHERE coursename='PHP')) as PHPN,
(SELECT COUNT(s.studentid)
FROM students s INNER JOIN student_course sc
ON s.studentid=sc.studentid
AND sc.courseid in
(SELECT courseid
FROM courses
WHERE coursename='Pearl')) as PEARLN,
(SELECT COUNT(s.studentid)
FROM students s INNER JOIN student_course sc
ON s.studentid=sc.studentid
AND sc.courseid in
(SELECT courseid
FROM courses
WHERE coursename='CSS')) as CSSN,
(SELECT COUNT(s.studentid)
FROM students s INNER JOIN student_course sc
ON s.studentid=sc.studentid
AND sc.courseid in
(SELECT courseid
FROM courses
WHERE coursename='Assembly')) as ASMN,
(SELECT COUNT(s.studentid)
FROM students s INNER JOIN student_course sc
ON s.studentid=sc.studentid
AND sc.courseid in
(SELECT courseid
FROM courses
WHERE coursename='JavaScript')) as JSN,

```
(SELECT COUNT(s.studentid)
FROM students s INNER JOIN student_course sc
ON s.studentid=sc.studentid
AND sc.courseid in
(SELECT courseid
FROM courses
WHERE coursename='python')) as PYTN,
(SELECT COUNT(s.studentid)
FROM students s INNER JOIN student_course sc
ON s.studentid=sc.studentid
AND sc.courseid in
(SELECT courseid
FROM courses
WHERE coursename='Unix')) as UNIXN
FROM students
```

Output:

TOTAL	CN	HTMLN	JN	VBN	PHPN	PEARLN	CSSN	ASMN	JSN
12	3	3	5	7	1	7	1	1	3

PYTN	UNIXN
1	0

We created a query monster and it is working! Are you proud? You must be!

Almost the same result can be achieved by using the following short query:

```
SELECT c.coursename as course,
count(s.studentid) as "students number" from students s INNER JOIN
student_course sc ON s.studentid=sc.studentid INNER JOIN courses c
ON sc.courseid=c.courseid GROUP BY c.coursename ORDER BY
count(s.studentid) desc
```

course	students number
Pearl	7
Visual Basic	7
Java	5
C++	3
JavaScript	3
HTML	3
Unix	1

SQL	1
Python	1
Assembly	1
PHP	1

The difference is the above query will return only number of students for the courses which have at least 1 student. If no student attends a course then the record about the course will not be returned. Why?

Because INNER JOIN returns only records with values that match in both tables.

The monster query returns all courses even if no one student attends a course.

APPENDIX

Create Table Statements for MySQL Database

CREATE TABLE students (
studentid int(11) NOT NULL auto_increment,
lastname varchar(15) NOT NULL default",
firstname varchar(15) NOT NULL default",
email varchar(30) NOT NULL default ",
phone varchar(30) NOT NULL default ",
age int(11) NOT NULL,
gender varchar (6) NOT NULL default ",
startdate date default NULL,
PRIMARY KEY (studentid)
)

CREATE TABLE courses (
courseid int(11) NOT NULL auto_increment,
coursename varchar(50) NOT NULL default ",
hours int(11) NOT NULL default '100',
cost float NOT NULL default '1000',
PRIMARY KEY (courseid)
) ENGINE=MyISAM AUTO_INCREMENT=1 DEFAULT CHARSET=latin1

CREATE TABLE student_course (
studentcourseid int(11) NOT NULL auto_increment,
studentid int(11) NOT NULL,
courseid int(11) NOT NULL,

```
paid tinyint(1) NOT NULL default '0',
PRIMARY KEY (studentcourseid)
)    ENGINE=MyISAM    AUTO_INCREMENT=1    DEFAULT
CHARSET=latin1
```

```
CREATE TABLE teachers (
teacherid int(11) NOT NULL auto_increment,
lastname varchar(15) NOT NULL default '',
firstname varchar(15) NOT NULL default '',
email varchar(30) NOT NULL default '',
phone varchar(20) NOT NULL default '',
hiredate date default NULL,
rate int(11) NOT NULL default '30',
PRIMARY KEY (teacherid)
)    ENGINE=MyISAM    AUTO_INCREMENT=1    DEFAULT
CHARSET=latin1
```

```
create table cars(
cid int(11) NOT NULL auto_increment,
teacherid int(11),
cmake varchar(20),
cyear varchar(4),
PRIMARY KEY(cid)
);
```

Create Table Statements for Oracle Database

```
CREATE TABLE cars(
cid NUMBER(11),
teacherid NUMBER(11),
cmake VARCHAR2(20),
cyear VARCHAR2(4),
CONSTRAINT pk_cars PRIMARY KEY (cid)
);
```

Oracle does not have auto-number data type as MS Access does or auto_increment attribute as MySQL does.

You have to create a sequence object that will keep track of record number.

Also, Oracle date format is different than MySQL date format.

For example, 1/1/2011 in MySQL DATE format is '2011-01-01', in Oracle DATE format is '01-JAN-11'.

If you want to insert your records in Oracle using MySQL date format then you can change session by executing the following command in SQL/PLUS:

alter session set nls_date_format='YYYY-MM-DD';

Let us create a sequence for the cars table. Actually, tables and sequences are not linked. You have to remember which sequence you use for the table. That is why it is convenient to name a sequence the same way as you name the table.

```
create sequence cars_seq
start with 1
increment by 1
nomaxvalue;
```

When you are inserting new record in the car table, you have to use cars_seq.nextval as a value for new record ID.

INSERT INTO cars VALUES (cars_seq.nextval, 1, 'Ford', '2007');

```
CREATE TABLE students (
studentid NUMBER(11),
lastname VARCHAR2(20),
firstname VARCHAR2(20),
email VARCHAR2(50),
phone VARCHAR2(20),
age NUMBER(11),
gender VARCHAR2(20),
startdate DATE,
CONSTRAINT pk_students PRIMARY KEY (studentid)
)
```

```
create sequence students_seq
start with 1
increment by 1
nomaxvalue;
```

INSERT INTO students VALUES (students_seq.nextval, 'Holden', 'Michael', 'mHolden@yahoo.com', '272-321-2222', 30, 'male', '2010-12-01');

```
CREATE TABLE courses (
courseid NUMBER(11),
coursename VARCHAR2(20),
hours NUMBER(11),
```

```
cost NUMBER(11),
CONSTRAINT pk_courses PRIMARY KEY (courseid)
);

create sequence courses_seq
    start with 1
    increment by 1
    nomaxvalue;

    INSERT INTO `courses` VALUES (courses_seq.nextval, 'Visual Basic',
360, 1999.95);
    CREATE TABLE student_course (
    studentcourseid NUMBER(11),
    studentid NUMBER(11),
    courseid NUMBER(11),
    paid NUMBER(11),
    CONSTRAINT pk_std_courses PRIMARY KEY (studentcourseid)
    );

    create sequence std_courses_seq
    start with 1
    increment by 1
    nomaxvalue;

    INSERT INTO student_course VALUES (std_courses_seq.nextval, 12,
9, 1);

    CREATE TABLE teachers (
    teacherid NUMBER(11),
    lastname VARCHAR2(20),
    firstname VARCHAR2(20),
    email VARCHAR2(20),
    phone VARCHAR2(20),
    hiredate DATE,
    rate NUMBER(11),
    CONSTRAINT pk_teachers PRIMARY KEY (teacherid)
    );

    create sequence teachers_seq
    start with 1
    increment by 1
    nomaxvalue;
```

INSERT INTO `teachers` VALUES (teachers_seq.nextval, 'Smith', 'John', 'johns@amail.com', '727-123-1234', '2000-07-01', 62);

```
CREATE TABLE schedule (
scheduleid NUMBER(11),
courseid NUMBER(11),
teacherid NUMBER(11),
starttime TIME,
endtime TIME,
startdate DATE,
CONSTRAINT pk_schedule PRIMARY KEY (scheduleid)
);
```

```
create sequence schedule_seq
start with 1
increment by 1
nomaxvalue;
```
INSERT INTO schedule VALUES (schedule_seq.nextval, 2, 1, '09:00:00', '15:00:00', '2010-01-11');

Oracle Cheat Sheet for Developers.

This tutorial is about most often used PL/SQL statements.

Please read Oracle documentation for comprehensive reference:

Oracle Database.
http://docs.oracle.com/en/database/database.html

Introduction to Oracle database.
http://docs.oracle.com/database/121/CNCPT/intro.htm#CNCPT001

Server-Side Programming: PL/SQL and Java.
http://docs.oracle.com/database/121/CNCPT/srvrside.htm#CNCPT1758

PL/SQL To display all tables:

SELECT TABLE_NAME, OWNER from SYS.ALL_TABLES order by OWNER, TABLE_NAME

Create table statement:

```
CREATE TABLE teachers (
teacherid NUMBER (11),
last_name VARCHAR2 (20),
first_name VARCHAR2 (20),
email VARCHAR2 (50),
phone VARCHAR2 (20),
hiredate DATE,
rate NUMBER (3),
CONSTRAINT pk_teachers PRIMARY KEY (teacherid)
);
```

PLS/SQL To display column names for teachers table:

```
SELECT COLUMN_NAME
FROM all_tab_columns
WHERE TABLE_NAME = 'teachers';
```

Data type for numeric data teacherid is NUMBER (11). 11 means that number can be 11 digits long (99,999,999,999). This field can store only whole numbers. If you try to insert 9.4 it will be rounded to 9. If you try to insert 9.5 It will rounded to 10.

Fixed-point number can be specified as NUMBER(p,s) where p - is the precision, or the total number of digits and s - is the scale, or the number of digits to the right of the decimal point.

Original Number	Number Format	Stored Number
9999999.99	NUMBER	9999999.99
9999999.99	NUMBER(7.1)	9999999.9
9999999.99	NUMBER(7,2)	9999999.99
9999999.44	NUMBER(7)	9999999
9999998.55	NUMBER(7)	9999999
9999999.99	NUMBER(7,-2)	9999900

Data type for alphabetical data last_name is VARCHAR2 (20). 20 is the maximum length of the string that can be stored. If you try to save longer string Oracle returns an error.

VARCHAR2 maximum length is 4000.

If you need to store longer text you can use CLOB. CLOB maximum size is 4 gigabytes. Using CLOB data type has some disadvantages. You cannot sort by CLOB column and cannot use LIKE for searching by CLOB data.

For example, if we had bio column in the teachers table and used CLOB as data type, we could not use such query as: "SELECT * FROM teachers where bio LIKE '%immigrated%'; to search teachers that were immigrated in US. But we can use query with LIKE for searching by last name or 'first name. For example: "SELECT * FROM TEACHERS WHERE LAST_NAME LIKE '%e%' returns all teachers which have 'e' in their last name.

Hiredate is DATE data type. Oracle's Date includes century, year, month, day, hour, minute, and second. Default date format is DD-MON-YY. For example, Christmas in 2015 date is 25-DEC-15. To insert date to oracle you have to convert date format to Oracle default format or change date column format:

ALTER SESSION SET nls_date_format='DD/MM/YYYY';

After that you can insert date in regular format: 'DD/MM/YYYY;
SYSDATE function returns the current date and time.

SELECT TO_CHAR
    (SYSDATE, 'MM-DD-YYYY HH24:MI:SS') "NOW"
    FROM DUAL;

TO_CHART function convert date and time to string.
12-25-2015 16:05:30

PLS/SQL statement to create sequence:

create sequence teachers _seq
start with 1
increment by 1
nomaxvalue;

You may start sequence from any number and increment by any number and instead of nomaxvalue Set MAXVALUE to any number, set MINVALUE to any number or set to NOMINVALUE.

A sequence can be used for auto-increment a table id number field. The sequence name has nothing to do with table name. It can be any. To insert a record into a table using the sequence use the sequence next value: teachers _seq.nextval.

INSERT INTO teachers (teacherid, last_name, first_name, email, phone, hiredate, rate)
    VALUES (teachers_seq.nextval,

```
'Smith',
'John',
'johns@amail.com',
'727-123-1234',
'10-JUN-15',
62);
```

If hiredate is current date you can use SYSDATE function.

```
INSERT INTO teachers (teacherid, last_name, first_name, email,
phone, hiredate, rate)
    VALUES (teachers_seq.nextval,
        'Smith',
        'John',
        'johns@amail.com',
        '727-123-1234',
        SYSDATE,
        82);
    Or:
```

```
INSERT INTO teachers (teacherid, last_name, first_name, email,
phone, hiredate, rate)
    VALUES (teachers_seq.nextval,
        'Smith',
        'John',
        'johns@amail.com',
        '727-123-1234',
        TRUNC(SYSDATE),
        62) ;
```

The SYSDATE will insert date and time, while TRUNC (SYSDATE) will insert only date.

You can use TIMESTAMP with date format 'YYYY-MM-DD HH:MM:SS':

```
INSERT INTO teachers (teacherid, last_name, first_name, email,
phone, hiredate, rate)
    VALUES (teachers_seq.nextval,
        'Smith',
        'John',
        'johns@amail.com',
```

```
'727-123-1234',
TIMESTAMP '2015-06-25 01:22:43',
        62);
```

If you want to insert data in all table's fields then it is not necessary to list all of them as in query above. Instead you can write:

```
INSERT INTO teachers
VALUES (teachers_seq.nextval,
    'Smith',
    'John',
    'johns@amail.com',
    '727-123-1234',
    TIMESTAMP '2015-06-25 01:22:43',
        62);
```

If you want to insert data in some of the fields you should list only that few fields:

```
INSERT INTO teachers (teacherid, last_name, first_name)
VALUES (teachers_seq.nextval,
    'Smith',
    'John');
```

You can copy in a table data from the other table that have the same data structure. For example if you create a second table teachers2 then you can insert data in table 2 from table 1.

```
INSERT INTO TEACHERS2
SELECT *
FROM TEACHERS.
```

If you have a sequence teachers2_seq for teachers2 table, you have to remember that when you copied data from the teachers table to the teachers2 table using statement above, teachers2_seq current number was not changed and if then you will try to insert a new record into the teachers2 table using the teachers2_seq.nextval, you will get an error because the teachers2_seq.nextval will be still equal to 1 and the record with id=1 is already exists in the teachers2 table.

If you copied, for example, 100 records you have to drop current teachers2_seq sequence and create it again with the starting number greater than 100.

You can find out maximum id number from the teachers2 table:

```
SELECT MAX (teacherid)
FROM teachers2;
```

Let's say, you get 100. Then you have to create a new sequence that starting from a number greater than 100, for example 120.

```
DROP SEQUENCE teachers2_seq;
```

```
CREATE SEQUENCE teachers2 _seq
start with 120
increment by 1
nomaxvalue;
```

Modifying Table

Let's add the address column to the teachers table and make it 100 characters long. Use the following PL/SQL:

```
ALTER TABLE teachers add address VARCHAR2 (100);
```

Let's say, you want to break address to separate fields: street, city, state, zip. For that you have to add additional columns to the teachers table using the following command:

```
ALTER TABLE teachers
ADD (city VARCHAR2 (20),
state VARCHAR2 (2),
zip VARCHAR2 (5)
);
```

Now you have to rename address column to street using the following command:

```
ALTER TABLE teachers
RENAME COLUMN address to street;
```

The street column is 100 characters long. Let's change its length.

```
ALTER TABLE teachers
MODIFY street VARCHAR2 (40);
```

Now, street field is 40 characters long.

Let's rename the teachers table name to instructors:

```
ALTER TABLE teachers
RENAME to instructors;
Rename sequence:
RENAME teachers_seq to instructors_seq;
```

In SQL query, a string and date/time values should be included in the single quotation marks. If string of text includes inside a single quotation mark then you need to add to the inside quotation mark one more quotation mark to get two single quotation marks. For example, the string 'St Mary's Street' should be inserted as 'St Mary''s Street'.

```
INSERT INTO instructors (instructorid, last_name, first_name, email,
phone, hiredate, rate, street, city, STATE, zip)
VALUES (instructors_seq.nextval,
    'Smith',
    'John',
    'johnsm@amail.com',
    '727-123-1234',
    TIMESTAMP '2015-06-25',
        92,
        '123 St Mary''s Street',
        'Dunedin',
        'FL',
        '34697');
```

You can alter a sequence with PL/SQL:

```
ALTER SEQUENCE teachers INCREMENT BY 100;
```

```
ALTER SEQUENCE teachers INCREMENT BY -100;
```

If you want to know a sequence next value use PL/SQL:

```
SELECT instructors_seq.nexval FROM DUAL;
```

To display all sequences that belong to a current user.

```
SELECT sequence_name FROM USER SEQUENCES;
```

To create a copy of a table for a different user

```
CREATE USER my_user IDENTIFIED BY password;

GRANT SELECT ON instructors TO my_user;

CREATE TABLE instructors_backups AS
SELECT *
FROM instructors;
```

To drop table use the following PL/SQL command:

```
DROP TABLE instructors;
```

Call Oracle procedures or functions

The difference between functions and procedures is that Oracle functions returns only one value, while procedures can have multiple OUT parameters.

Example 1.Oracle procedure insert_instructor:

```
CREATE OR REPLACE PROCEDURE insert_instructor (
pLast_name IN VARCHAR2, pFirst_name IN VARCHAR2,
pEmail IN VARCHAR2, pPhone IN VARCHAR2, pHiredate IN DATE,
pRate IN NUMBER, pStreet IN VARCHAR2, pCity IN VARCHAR2,
pState IN VARCHAR2, pZip IN VARCHAR2, instructor_id OUT NUMBER,) IS

-- declare variable for inserted record id.
vl_instructor_id NUMBER;

BEGIN -- add a record to the instructors table.

INSERT INTO instructors (instructorid, last_name,
first_name, email, phone, hiredate, rate, street, city, STATE, zip))
VALUES (instructors_seq.nextval,
    pLast_name pFirst_name,
    pEmail,
    pPhone,
    pHiredate,
    pRate,
    pStreet,
    pCity,
```

```
        pState,
        pZip) RETURNING instructorid INTO v_instructor_id;

    instructor_id:= vl_instructor_id;

    RETURN;

    END insert_instructor;
```

Call procedure in PL/SQL:

```
BEGIN
     insert_instructor  ('Smith',  'John',  'johnsm@amail.com',  '727-123-
1234',
     '25-JUN-15', 92, '123 St Mary"s Street', 'Dunedin', 'FL', '34697');

END;
```

Call Oracle procedure in PHP:

```php
<?php
$myuser="smithjohn ";
$mypassword="Practice7 ";
$mydb="(DESCRIPTION = (ADDRESS =
(PROTOCOL = TCP)(HOST = my_host)(PORT myport))
(CONNECT_DATA        =        (SERVICE_NAME        =
my_oracle_user.my_host)))";

    if(!$myconn=oci_connect($myuser, $mypassword, $mydb))
    {
       $e = oci_error();
    echo "if not connection<br>";

      echo htmlentities($e['message']);
    }
    else
    {
    $query1="BEGIN INSERT_INSTRUCTOR(:last_name, :first_name,
    :email, :phone, :hiredate, :rate, :street, :city,
    :state, :zip, :instructorid); end;";

    $stmt1 = oci_parse($myconn, $query1);
```

```
$lastname='Williams';
$firstname='Bob';
$email="bobw@yahoo.com";
$phone="727-123-1234";
$hiredate="01-JAN-15";
$rate=80;
$street="423 Druid Rd."
$city="Clearwater";
$state="FL";
$zip="33756";

oci_bind_by_name($stmt1, ":instructorid", $ instructorid, 10);
oci_bind_by_name($stmt1, ":lastname", $lastname);
oci_bind_by_name($stmt1, ":firstname", $firstname);
oci_bind_by_name($stmt1, ":phone", $phone);
oci_bind_by_name($stmt1, ":hiredate", $hiredate);
oci_bind_by_name($stmt1, ":rate", $rate);
oci bind_by_name($stmt1, ":street", $street);
oci_bind_by_name($stmt1, ":city", $city);
oci_bind_by_name($stmt1, ": state ", $ state);
oci_bind_by_name($stmt1, ":zip", $zip);

$er1=oci_execute($stmt1);

    if(!$er1)
    {
    $e = oci_error($stmt1);
    echo $e['message'];
    }

                $ret1=oci_commit($myconn);

echo "Instructor ID=". $instructorid;

} //if connected
```

Example 2. Oracle Function insert_instructor.

```
CREATE OR REPLACE FUNCTION insert_instructor (
pLast_name IN VARCHAR2, pFirst_name IN VARCHAR2, pEmail
IN VARCHAR2,
    pPhone IN VARCHAR2, pHiredate IN DATE, pRate IN NUMBER,
```

pStreet IN VARCHAR2, pCity IN VARCHAR2, pState IN VARCHAR2,
pZip IN VARCHAR2) RETURN number IS RESULT number;

```
BEGIN
INSERT INTO instructors (instructorid, last_name, first_name,
email, phone, hiredate, rate, street, city, STATE, zip)

VALUES (instructors_seq.nextval,
      pLast_name,
      pFirst_name,
      pEmail,
      pPhone,
      pHiredate,
      pRate,
      pStreet,
      pCity,
      pState,
      pZip) RETURNING instructorid INTO RESULT;
```

Call insert_instructor Oracle function in PHP

```php
<?php

$query2="BEGIN :result := INSERT_INSTRUCTOR(
:last_name, :first_name, :email, :phone, :hiredate,
:rate, :street, :city, :state, :zip); end;";

$stmt2 = oci_parse ($myconn, $query2);

$lastname='Willams';
$firstname='Bob';
$email="bobw@yahoo.com";
$phone="727-123-1234";
$hiredate="01-JAN-15";
$rate=80;
$street="423 Druid Rd.";
$city="Clearwater";
$state="FL";
$zip="33756";

oci_bind_by_name($stmt2, ":result", $result, 10);
oci_bind_by_name($stmt2, ":lastname", $lastname);
```

```
oci_bind_by_name($stmt2, ":firstname", $firstname);
oci_bind_by_name($stmt2, ":phone", $phone);
oci_bind_by_name($stmt2, ":hiredate", $hiredate);
oci_bind_by_name($stmt2, ":rate", $rate);
oci_bind_by_name($stmt2, ":street", $street);
oci_bind_by_name($stmt2, ":city", $city);
oci_bind_by_name($stmt2, ":state ", $state);
oci_bind_by_name($stmt2, ":zip", $zip);

$er2=oci_execute($stmt2);

   if(!$er2)
   {
 $e = oci_error($stmt2);
 echo $e['message'];
 }

  $ret2=oci_commit ($myconn);

echo "Instructor ID=". $result."<br>";
?>
```

Example 3. Oracle procedure update_hiredate.

This procedure takes in three parameters: last name and first name, new hire date and takes out one parameter instructorid.

```
CREATE OR REPLACE PROCEDURE update_hiredate (
plastname IN VARCHAR2, pfirstname IN VARCHAR2,
pnew_hiredate IN DATE, pinstructor_id OUT NUMBER)
IS lv_instructorid NUMBER;

BEGIN
UPDATE instructors
SET hiredate= pnew_hiredate
WHERE firstname=pfirstname
  AND lastname=plastname
  RETURNING instructorid INTO lv_instructorid;

 pinstructor_id:= lv_instructorid;

RETURN;
```

END update_hiredate;

Call update_hiredate Oracle procedure with PHP

```php
<?php
……
$query3="BEGIN update_hiredate (:last_name,
:first_name, :new_hiredate, :instructor_id) ;end;";

$stmt3 = oci_parse ($myconn, $query3);

$lastname="Barry";
$firstname="John";
$new_hiredate="07-FEB-14";

$istructor_id=0;
oci_bind_by_name($stmt3, ": instructor_id ", $istructor_id, 10);
oci_bind_by_name($stmt3, ":last_name", $lastname);
oci_bind_by_name($stmt3, ":first_name", $firstname);
oci_bind_by_name($stmt3, ":new_hiredate", $new_hiredate);

$er3=oci_execute($stmt3);

    if(!$er3)
    {
    $e = oci_error($stmt3);
    echo $e['message'];
    }

      $ret3=oci_commit($myconn);

echo "Instructor_ID=". $istructor_id."<br>";
```

Example 4. Oracle function update_hiredate.

```
CREATE OR REPLACE FUNCTION update_hiredate (
plastname IN VARCHAR2,
pfirstname IN VARCHAR2, pnew_hiredate IN DATE)
RETURN DATE IS RESULT DATE;

 BEGIN
UPDATE instructors
SET hiredate= pnew_hiredate
```

```
WHERE firstname=pfirstname
  AND lastname=plastname RETURNING hiredate INTO RESULT;

 RETURN (RESULT);

 END update_hiredate;
```

Call update_hiredate function with PHP

```php
<?php
......
$sql4="BEGIN: result := update_hiredate (
:last_name, :first_name, :new_hiredate) ; end;"

$stmt4 = oci_parse ($myconn, $sql4);

$lastname="Barry";
$firstname="John";
$new_hiredate="07-MAR-14";

oci_bind_by_name($stmt4, ": result ", $result, 10);
oci_bind_by_name($stmt4, ":last_name", $lastname);
oci_bind_by_name($stmt4, ":first_name", $firstname);
oci_bind_by_name($stmt4, ":new_hiredate", $new_hiredate);

$er4=oci_execute ($stmt4);

     If (!$er4)
     {
     $e = oci_error($stmt4);
     echo $e['message'];
     }

   $ret4=oci_commit ($myconn);

   echo "New hire date=".  $result."<br>";
```

Example 5. Oracle function return_hiredate.

```
CREATE OR REPLACE FUNCTION return_hiredate (
pfirstname IN VARCHAR2, plastname IN VARCHAR2)
RETURN DATE IS RESULT DATE;
```

```
 BEGIN
SELECT hiredate INTO RESULT
FROM instructors
WHERE lastname = plastname
  AND firstname = pfirstname;

 RETURN (RESULT);

 END return_hiredate;
```

Call return_hiredate function with PHP

```
$query5="BEGIN  :result  :=  return_hiredate(:firstname,  :lastname);
end;";

$lastname="Barry";
$firstname="John";

  $stmt5 = oci_parse ($myconn, $query5);

  oci_bind_by_name ($stmt5, ":result", $result,50);
  oci_bind_by_name ($stm5t, ":lastname", $lastname);
  oci_bind_by_name ($stmt5, ":firstname", $firstname);

      $er5=oci_execute($stmt5);

      if(!$er5)
      {
      $e = oci_error($stmt5);
      echo $e['message'];
      }

      $ret5=oci_commit($myconn);

      echo "hire date=".$result."<br>";
}
?>
```

Example 6. Oracle procedure return_hiredate.

CREATE OR REPLACE PROCEDURE return_hiredate (

pfirstname IN VARCHAR2, plastname IN VARCHAR2,
pHiredate OUT DATE) IS lv_hiredate DATE;

```
BEGIN
SELECT hiredate INTO lv_hiredate
FROM instructors
WHERE lastname = plastname
 AND firstname = pfirstname;

 pHiredate := lv_hiredate;

 RETURN;

 END return_hiredate;
```

Call return_hiredate procedure with PHP

```php
<?php

 $query6="BEGIN return_hiredate(:firstname, :lastname, :hiredate);

end;";

$firstname='john';

$lastname='smith';

$hiredate="";

$stmt6=oci_parse($myconn, $query6);

oci_bind_by_name($stmt6, ":hiredate", $hiredate, 20);

oci_bind_by_name($stmt6, ":lastname", $lastname);

oci_bind_by_name($stmt6, ":firstname", $firstname);

 $er6=oci_execute($stmt6);

if(!$er6)
 {
$e = oci_error($stmt6); echo $e['message'];
 }
```

```php
$ret6=oci_commit($myconn);
echo "Hire date=".$hiredate."<br>";
}

?>
```

Example 7. Oracle procedure delete_instructor.

```
CREATE OR REPLACE PROCEDURE delete_instructor(
plastname IN OUT VARCHAR2, pfirstname IN VARCHAR2)
IS lv_lastname VARCHAR2(20);

 BEGIN
DELETE
FROM instructors
WHERE lastname=plastname
  AND firstname=pfirstname returning lastname INTO lv_lastname;

plastname:=lv_lastname;

RETURN;

END delete_instructor;
```

Call delete_instructor procedure with PHP

```php
<?php
$sql7="BEGIN delete_instructor(:last_name, :first_name); end;";

$istmt7 = oci_parse($myconn, $sql7);

$last_name='Barry';
$first_name='John';

oci_bind_by_name($istmt7, ":last_name", $last_name);
oci_bind_by_name($istmt7, ":first_name", $first_name);

$er7=oci_execute($istmt7);
    if(!$er7)
    {
    $e = oci_error($stmt7);
    echo $e['message'];
    }
```

```php
$ret7=oci_commit($myconn);

echo "last name=". $last_name."<br>";

?>
```

Example 8. Oracle procedure get_instructors.

This procedure returns a cursor that can hold multiple records and fields.

```sql
CREATE OR REPLACE PROCEDURE get_instructors (
plastname IN VARCHAR2, mycurs OUT SYS_REFCURSOR)
IS

BEGIN OPEN mycurs
FOR
SELECT lastname,
    firstname,
    email,
    phone,
    hiredate,
    rate,
    street,
    city,
    STATE,
    zip
FROM instructors
WHERE lastname=plastname; END get_instructors;
```

Call get_instructors procedure with PHP

```php
<?php
.........
$curs = oci_new_cursor($myconn);

$lastname="Willams";
$query8="BEGIN get_instructors(:lastname, :curs ); end;";

$stmt8 = oci_parse($myconn, $query8);
oci_bind_by_name($stmt8, ":lastname", $lastname);
oci_bind_by_name($stmt8, ":curs", $curs, -1, OCI_B_CURSOR);
oci_execute($stmt8);
```

```
oci_execute($curs);

echo "Instructors Records:<br>";

while($row = oci_fetch_array($curs, OCI_NUM)) {
    $last_name=$row[0];
    $first_name=$row[1];
    $email=$row[2];
    $phone=$row[3];
    $hiredate=$row[4];
    $rate=$row[5];
    $street=$row[6];
    $city=$row[7];
    $state=$row[8];
    $zip=$row[9];

echo $last_name.' '.$first_name.' '.$email.'
'.$phone.' '.$hiredate.' '.$rate.' '.$street.'
'.$city.' '.$state.' '.$zip.'<br>';
}

oci_free_statement($stmt8);
oci_free_statement($curs);
oci_close($myconn);

?>
```

Example 9. Oracle procedure delete_instructor2.

This function returns a cursor.

```
CREATE OR REPLACE FUNCTION delete_instructor2(
plastname IN VARCHAR) RETURN SYS_REFCURSOR
AS my_cursor SYS_REFCURSOR;

 BEGIN

OPEN my_cursor
FOR
SELECT *
FROM instructors
WHERE lastname=plastname;
```

```sql
DELETE
FROM instructors
WHERE lastname=plastname;

 RETURN my_cursor;

 END delete_instructor2;
```

Call delete_instructor2 function with PHP

```php
<?php

$p_curs = oci_new_cursor($myconn);

$lastname="Tom";

$query9="BEGIN  :curs := delete_instructor2(:lastname); end;";

$stmt9 = oci_parse($myconn, $query9);
oci_bind_by_name($stmt9, ":lastname", $lastname);
oci_bind_by_name($stmt9, ':curs', $p_curs, -1, OCI_B_CURSOR);

   // Execute Statement
   oci_execute($stmt9);
   oci_execute($p_curs, OCI_DEFAULT);
echo "Deleted Records:<br>";
   while ($row = oci_fetch_array($p_curs, OCI_NUM)){
        $last_name=$row[0];
     $first_name=$row[1];
     $email=$row[2];
     $phone=$row[3];
     $hiredate=$row[4];
     $rate=$row[5];
     $street=$row[6];
     $city=$row[7];
     $state=$row[8];
     $zip=$row[9];

echo $last_name.' '.$first_name.' '.$email.'
'.$phone.' '.$hiredate.' '.$rate.' '.$street.'
'.$city.' '.$state.' '.$zip.'<br>';
     }
oci_commit ($myconn);
```

```
oci_free_statement($stmt9);
oci_free_statement($p_curs);
oci_close($myconn);
```

?>

CREATE TABLE Statements for MS Access Database

```
CREATE TABLE cars(
cid int,
teacherid int,
cmake text,
cyear text,
PRIMARY KEY(cid)
);
```

```
CREATE TABLE students (
studentid int,
lastname text,
firstname text,
email text,
phone text,
age int,
gender text,
startdate date,
PRIMARY KEY (studentid)
)
```

```
CREATE TABLE courses (
courseid int,
coursename text,
hours int,
cost int,
PRIMARY KEY (courseid)
);
```

```
CREATE TABLE student_course (
studentcourseid int,
studentid int,
courseid int,
paid int,
PRIMARY KEY (studentcourseid)
```

);

```
CREATE TABLE teachers (
teacherid int,
lastname text,
firstname text,
email text,
phone text,
hiredate date,
rate int,
PRIMARY KEY (teacherid)
);

CREATE TABLE schedule (
scheduleid int,
courseid int,
teacherid int,
starttime time,
endtime time,
startdate date,
PRIMARY KEY (scheduleid)
);

CREATE TABLE test_grades(
tgid int,
grade int,
studentid int,
courseid int,
PRIMARY KEY (tgid)
);
```

Homework

1. Find students' emails whose firstname is Michael?

2. Find email and phone number for student, whose last name is Johnson.

3. Find age and gender for students whose start dates were after 12/03/2010.

4. Find students whose start dates were between 12/03/2010 and 12/31/2010.

5. Find students whose start dates were after 12/03/2010 but before

12/31/2010.

6.Find students whose start dates were after 12/03/2010 and whose age is less than 25.

7.Find students whose start dates were after 12/03/2010 and whose age greater than 21 and less than 25

8. Find students whose start dates were after 12/01/2010 and age less than 30 and greater than 23.

9. Find teachers who were hired after 12/01/2010.

10. Find teachers who were hired after 01/01/2011.

11. Display hire dates for all teachers.

12. Find last name and hire date for teachers whose first name is Michael.

13. What is first name and hire date for teacher Ross?

14. What is phone number for teacher Kelly?

15. What is phone number for teacher Jefferson?

16. What is hire date and phone number for teacher Mr. Jefferson?

17. What is first name and phone number for teacher Mr. Murphy?

18. What is hire date and phone number for teacher Mr. Murphy?

19. What is a rate and phone number for teacher Mr. Murphy?

20. Which of teachers has the highest rate?

21. Which of teachers has the lowest rate?

22. Which teachers rate is above average?

23. Which teachers rate is below average?

24. Which students attend Smith classes?

25. Which students attend classes at evening?

26. Which students attend Java class at evening?

27. Which students attend HTML in the morning?

28. Which teachers teach JavaScript or PHP courses after noon?

29. Which teachers teach C++ or PHP?

30. Write the same query without sub query.

31. Which teachers teach Visual Basic or Java afternoon?

32. Write the same query without sub query.

33. Which teacher teaches either PHP or CSS or both?

34.Write the same query without sub query.

35 Which teachers teach C++ or Java?

36. Write the same query without sub query.

37. Which teachers teach either C++, Java or Visual Basic?

38. Write the same query without sub query.

39.Which teacher teaches either HTML or CSS or both.

40 Write the same query without sub query.

Homework Answers

1.Find students' emails whose firstname is Michael?
SELECT email FROM students WHERE firstname='Michael'

email
michael@yahoo.com
jmichael@yahoo.com
holdent@yahoo.com

2.Find email and phone number for student, whose last name is Johnson
SELECT * FROM students WHERE lastname='Johnson'

email   phone
jmichael@yahoo.com   272-123-0111

3.Find age and gender for students whose start dates were after 12/03/2010
SELECT * FROM students WHERE startdate > '2010-12-03'

age   gender
23   female
23   female

4.Find students whose start dates were between 12/03/2010 and 12/31/2010
SELECT firstname, lastname FROM students WHERE startdate between '2010-12-03' AND '2010-12-31'

Output:
firstname   lastname
Michael   Petrov
Molly   James
Cindy   Brown
Julia   Barklay
Alison   Cremette
James   Folkner

5.Find students whose start dates were after 12/03/2010, but before 12/31/2010.
SELECT firstname, lastname FROM students WHERE startdate > '2010-12-03' AND startdate < '2010-12-31'

Output:
firstname   lastname
Cindy   Brown
Julia   Barklay

6.Find students whose start dates were after 12/03/2010 and whose age less than 25.

SELECT firstname, lastname FROM students WHERE startdate > '2010-12-01' AND age > 25

Output:
firstname   lastname
Molly   James

7.Find students whose start dates were after 12/03/2010 and whose age greater than 21 and less than 25.

SELECT firstname, lastname FROM students WHERE startdate > '2010-12-01' AND age >21 AND age <25

Output:
firstname   lastname
Cindy   Brown
Julia   Barklay

8. Find students whose start dates were after 12/01/2010 and age less than 30 and greater than 23.

SELECT firstname, lastname FROM students WHERE startdate > '2010-12-01' AND age >23 AND age <30

Output:
firstname   lastname
John   Williams
Alison   Cremette
James   Folkner

9. Find teachers who were hired after 12/01/2010.

SELECT firstname, lastname FROM teachers WHERE hiredate > '2010-12-01'

Output:
firstname   lastname
John   Niven
Christine   Merry

10. Find teachers who were hired after 01/01/2011.

SELECT firstname, lastname FROM teachers WHERE hiredate > '2011-01-01'

Output:
firstname	lastname
John	Niven
Christine	Merry

11. Display hire date for all teachers.
SELECT hiredate FROM teachers

Output:
hiredate
2000-07-01
2005-07-01
2003-09-01
2000-07-01
2007-09-01
2011-09-01
2011-09-06
2009-09-01
2010-08-09
2008-07-03
2010-09-02

12 Find last name and hire date for teachers whose first name is Michael.
SELECT lastname, hiredate FROM teachers WHERE firstname='Michael'

Output:
lastname	hiredate
Murphy	2000-07-01
Ross	2010-08-09
Kelly	2008-07-03

13. What is first name and hire date for teacher Ross?

SELECT firstname, hiredate FROM teachers WHERE lastname='Ross'

Output:
firstname   hiredate
Michael   2010-08-09

14. What is phone number for teacher Kelly?

SELECT phone FROM teachers WHERE lastname='Kelly'

phone   727-098-1237

15. What is phone number for teacher Jefferson?

SELECT phone FROM teachers WHERE lastname='Jefferson'

phone   727-987-1234

16. What is hire date and phone number for teacher Mr. Jefferson?

SELECT   hiredate,   phone   FROM   teachers   WHERE
lastname='Jefferson'

hiredate   phone
2005-07-01   727-987-1234

17. What is first name and phone number for teacher Mr. Murphy?
SELECT   firstname,   phone   FROM   teachers   WHERE
lastname='Murphy'
 Output:
firstname   phone
Michael   910-987-1234

18. What is hire date and phone number for teacher Mr. Murphy?
SELECT hiredate, phone FROM teachers WHERE lastname='Murphy'

Output:
hiredate   phone
2000-07-01   910-987-1234

19. What is a rate and phone number for teacher Mr. Murphy?
SELECT rate, phone FROM teachers WHERE lastname='Murphy'

Output:
rate   phone

61   910-987-1234

20. Which of teachers has the highest rate?
SELECT firstname, lastname, rate FROM teachers WHERE rate=(SELECT MAX(rate) FROM teachers)

Output:
firstname	lastname	rate
John	Smith	62

21. Which of teachers has the lowest rate?
SELECT firstname, lastname, rate FROM teachers WHERE rate=(SELECT MIN(rate) FROM teachers)

Output:
firstname	lastname	rate
John	Niven	20
Michael	Ross	20

22. Which teachers rate is above average?
SELECT firstname, lastname, rate FROM teachers WHERE rate > (SELECT AVG(rate) FROM teachers)

Output:
firstname	lastname	rate
John	Smith	62
John	Jefferson	51
James	Barry	51
Michael	Murphy	61
Julia	Williams	51

23. Which teachers rate is below average?
SELECT firstname, lastname, rate FROM teachers WHERE rate < (SELECT AVG(rate) FROM teachers)

Output:
firstname	lastname	rate
John	Niven	20
Christine	Merry	30
Greg	Gerald	30
Michael	Ross	20
Michael	Kelly	25
Norm	Karon	30

24. Which students attend Smith classes?

```
SELECT DISTINCT s.firstname, s.lastname
FROM students s
INNER JOIN student_course sc
ON s.studentid=sc.studentid
INNER JOIN schedule h
ON sc.courseid=h.courseid
WHERE h.teacherid in
(SELECT teacherid
FROM teachers
WHERE lastname='Smith')
ORDER BY s.lastname, s.firstname
```

Output:

firstname	lastname
Molly	James
Michael	Johnson
Holly	Michaels
Michael	Petrov
Michael	Holden

25. Which students attend classes at evening?

```
SELECT DISTINCT s.firstname, s.lastname
FROM students s INNER JOIN student_course sc
ON s.studentid=sc.studentid
INNER JOIN schedule h
ON sc.courseid=h.courseid
WHERE h.starttime >'12:00:00'
ORDER BY s.lastname, s.firstname
```

The same query for MS Access. Date and Time data type enclosed in # chars.

Two tables join enclosed in parentheses.

```
SELECT DISTINCT s.firstname, s.lastname
FROM (students s INNER JOIN student_course sc
ON s.studentid=sc.studentid)
INNER JOIN schedule h
```

ON sc.courseid=h.courseid
WHERE starttime > #12:00:00#
ORDER BY s.lastname, s.firstname

Output:

firstname	lastname
Julia	Barklay
Lee	George
Cindy	Brown
Ryan	Brown
Alison	Cremette
James	Folkner
Molly	James
Michael	Johnson
Holly	Michaels
Michael	Petrov
Michael	Holden
John	Williams

26. Which students attend Java class at evening?

SELECT DISTINCT s.firstname, s.lastname
FROM students s INNER JOIN student_course sc
ON s.studentid=sc.studentid
INNER JOIN schedule h
ON sc.courseid=h.courseid
AND h.starttime >'12:00:00'
AND h.courseid in
(SELECT courseid
FROM courses
WHERE coursename='Java')
ORDER BY s.lastname, s.firstname

Output:

firstname	lastname
Michael	Holden
Molly	James
Michael	Johnson
Holly	Michaels
Michael	Petrov

27. Which students attend HTML in the morning?

SELECT DISTINCT s.firstname, s.lastname
FROM students s INNER JOIN student_course sc
ON s.studentid=sc.studentid
INNER JOIN schedule h
ON sc.courseid=h.courseid
AND h.starttime < '12:00:00'
AND h.courseid in
(SELECT courseid
FROM courses
WHERE coursename='HTML')
ORDER BY s.lastname, s.firstname

Output:

firstname	lastname
Cindy	Brown
Ryan	Brown
Molly	James

28. Which teachers teach JavaScript or PHP courses after noon?

SELECT DISTINCT t.firstname, t.lastname
FROM teachers t INNER JOIN schedule s
ON t.teacherid=s.teacherid INNER JOIN courses c
ON s.courseid=c.courseid
AND (c.coursename='JavaScript' OR c.coursename='PHP')
AND s.starttime > '12:00:00'
ORDER BY t.lastname

Output:

firstname	lastname
John	Niven

29. Which teachers teach C++ or PHP?

```
SELECT DISTINCT t.firstname, t.lastname
FROM teachers t INNER JOIN schedule s
ON t.teacherid = s.teacherid AND s.courseid in
(SELECT courseid
FROM courses
WHERE coursename='C++'
OR coursename='PHP')
ORDER BY t.lastname, t.firstname
```

Output:

firstname	lastname
James	Barry
Norm	Karon
Michael	Kelly
Michael	Murphy

30. Write the same query without sub query.

```
SELECT DISTINCT t.firstname, t.lastname
FROM teachers t INNER JOIN schedule s
ON t.teacherid = s.teacherid INNER JOIN courses c
ON s.courseid=c.courseid
WHERE c.coursename='PHP'
OR c.coursename='C++'
ORDER BY t.lastname, t.firstname
```

Output:

firstname	lastname
James	Barry
Norm	Karon
Michael	Kelly
Michael	Murphy

31. Which teachers teach Visual Basic or Java afternoon?

```
SELECT DISTINCT t.firstname, t.lastname
FROM teachers t INNER JOIN schedule s
ON t.teacherid = s.teacherid
AND s.starttime > '12:00:00'
AND s.courseid in
(SELECT courseid
FROM courses
WHERE coursename='Visual Basic'
```

OR coursename='Java')
ORDER BY t.lastname, t.firstname

Output:
firstname   lastname
John   Jefferson
Christine   Merry
Michael   Ross

32. Write the same query without sub query

SELECT DISTINCT t.firstname, t.lastname
FROM teachers t INNER JOIN schedule s
ON t.teacherid = s.teacherid INNER JOIN courses c
ON s.courseid=c.courseid
AND (coursename='Visual Basic'
OR coursename='Java') AND s.starttime > '12:00:00'
ORDER BY t.lastname, t.firstname

Output:
firstname   lastname
John   Jefferson
Christine   Merry
Michael   Ross

33. Which teacher teaches either PHP or CSS or both?

SELECT t.firstname, t.lastname
FROM teachers t INNER JOIN schedule s
ON t.teacherid = s.teacherid
WHERE s.courseid in
(SELECT courseid
FROM courses
WHERE coursename='PHP')
OR s.courseid in
(SELECT courseid
FROM courses
WHERE coursename='CSS')
ORDER BY t.lastname, t.firstname

Output:

firstname	lastname
Michael	Murphy
Julia	Williams

34.Write the same query without sub query

```
SELECT DISTINCT t.firstname, t.lastname
FROM teachers t INNER JOIN schedule s
ON t.teacherid = s.teacherid INNER JOIN courses c
ON s.courseid=c.courseid
AND (coursename='PHP'
OR coursename='CSS' )
ORDER BY t.lastname, t.firstname
```

Output:

firstname	lastname
Michael	Murphy
Julia	Williams

35 Which teachers teach C++ or Java?

```
SELECT DISTINCT t.firstname, t.lastname
FROM teachers t INNER JOIN schedule s
ON t.teacherid = s.teacherid
AND s.courseid in
(SELECT courseid
FROM courses
WHERE coursename='C++'
OR coursename='Java' )
ORDER BY t.lastname, t.firstname
```

Output:

firstname	lastname
James	Barry
John	Jefferson
Norm	Karon
Michael	Kelly
Christine	Merry
John	Smith

36. Write the same query without sub query

SELECT DISTINCT t.firstname, t.lastname
FROM teachers t INNER JOIN schedule s
ON t.teacherid = s.teacherid INNER JOIN courses c
ON s.courseid=c.courseid
AND (coursename='C++'
OR coursename='Java')
ORDER BY t.lastname, t.firstname

Output:

firstname	lastname
James	Barry
John	Jefferson
Norm	Karon
Michael	Kelly
Christine	Merry
John	Smith

37. Which teachers teach either C++, Java or Visual Basic.

SELECT DISTINCT t.firstname, t.lastname
FROM teachers t INNER JOIN schedule s
ON t.teacherid = s.teacherid
AND s.courseid in
(SELECT courseid
FROM courses
WHERE coursename='C++'
OR coursename='Java'
OR coursename='Visual Basic')
ORDER BY t.lastname, t.firstname

Output:
firstname	lastname
James	Barry
John	Jefferson
Norm	Karon
Michael	Kelly
Christine	Merry

Michael   Ross
John   Smith

38. Write the same query without sub query

SELECT DISTINCT t.firstname, t.lastname
FROM teachers t INNER JOIN schedule s
ON t.teacherid = s.teacherid INNER JOIN courses c
ON s.courseid=c.courseid
AND (coursename='C++'
OR coursename='Java'
OR coursename='Visual Basic')
ORDER BY t.lastname, t.firstname

Output:

firstname	lastname
James	Barry
John	Jefferson
Norm	Karon
Michael	Kelly
Christine	Merry
Michael	Ross
John	Smith

39.Which teacher teaches either HTML of CSS or both.

SELECT t.firstname, t.lastname
FROM teachers t INNER JOIN schedule s
ON t.teacherid = s.teacherid
WHERE s.courseid in
(SELECT courseid
FROM courses
WHERE coursename='HTML')
OR s.courseid in
(SELECT courseid
FROM courses
WHERE coursename='CSS')
ORDER BY t.lastname, t.firstname

Output:

firstname	lastname
Julia	Williams
Julia	Williams

40 Write the same query without sub query.

```
SELECT t.firstname, t.lastname
FROM teachers t INNER JOIN schedule s
ON t.teacherid = s.teacherid INNER JOIN courses c
ON s.courseid=c.courseid
AND (coursename='CSS' or c.coursename='HTML')
ORDER BY t.lastname, t.firstname
```

Output:
firstname   lastname
Julia   Williams
Julia   Williams

Thanks for reading! If you found this book useful, I'd be very grateful if you'd post a short review on Amazon. Your support does make a difference. Your feedback helps me to make this book even better.

Would you be open to sharing how this book helped you? Your words will serve other readers to benefit from this work. If you'd prefer not to, that's all good as well. Thanks again for your support!

Thanks again for your support!

Resources:

www.learn-coding.today/tables.txt

Aggregate functions for MySQL
http://dev.mysql.com/doc/refman/5.1/en/group-by-functions.html
Oracle list of aggregate function
http://docs.oracle.com/cd/B19306_01/server.102/b14200/functions0
01.htm

My eBooks for Kindle on Amazon.com

Sergey Skudaev

C++ Programming By Examples
PHP Programming for Beginners

Roy Sawyer
Chemistry for Students and Parents
The Easiest Way To Understand Algebra
Geometry For Students and Parents

ABOUT THE AUTHOR

Sergey Skudaev is currently living in Arizona.
He obtained a Master's Degree in biology from a foreign University, where
he specialized in neuropsychology. He also has a degree in Computer
Science from BMCC, which he attained after moving to the States.
Since then, Sergey has been working as a software quality engineer and web
developer for a company in Florida.
He has more than ten years of teaching experience and a long-standing
interest in new computer technologies, psychology, and brain physiology.
When he has some time to relax, Sergey enjoys swimming in the ocean off
the Florida coast or going for walks with his dog on Window Rock trail. He
also enjoys traveling, particularly in the USA.
You can contact Sergey at support@learn-coding.today

www.ingramcontent.com/pod-product-compliance
Lightning Source LLC
Chambersburg PA
CBHW070106210526
45170CB00013B/764